Cover Design: Veronika Vana

Quilt: Nechama Cox

Creative Judaism
Partnering with God:

Insecurity and Love

Shaya Cohen & Susan Quinn

DEDICATION

To my mother, teacher, and intellectual guide,

Chana Berniker Cox.

May her memory be a blessing.

CONTENTS

HOW WE CAME TO WRITE THIS BOOK

This book started out as one person's labor of love—for God, Torah, Judaism and the Jewish people. Shaya Cohen, a practicing Jew, had already written one book about Judaism, *The Torah Manifesto*, and had written many essays that reflected his deepening understanding of what God wants from us. He decided to write another book, but in a different vein: a book that delivers an approachable and intriguing book for Jews who had fallen away from, or been estranged from Judaism, and for anyone who wanted to understand the soul and spirit of Judaism. His desire to communicate his love, dedication and joy to other Jews was resolute.

One day a friend of Shaya's mentioned that if he ever had a project that needed editing, he should call her. To Shaya, the message was clear: Susan Quinn, that friend, would be the quintessential Jew to partner with him on this new project. Although Susan was doubtful at first, Shaya explained that she was a profoundly talented and engaging writer who had returned to Judaism and was embracing her nascent faith with enthusiasm and curiosity. Who better to partner with him than a person with her limited training in Judaism, who could offer a beginner's perspective?

The project could have been challenging for both of us—two strong-minded, opinionated people. But our effort seemed to be blessed with camaraderie, dedication and the love of learning. There was only one hurdle to overcome: what would be the best way to have two people contribute, who were actively engaged in the book, without confusing the reader? We decided to take the following approach:

Since Shaya was the Torah expert, having studied Torah his entire life, he had many stories and experiences to relate based on his relationship to Judaism. It made sense for the book to be written in one voice, his voice. In no way do I want to lessen my (Susan's) own contribution, the challenging task of integrating over 100 essays and an already published book, and making sure that I understood not only the content, but the message that Shaya meant to share. I learned a great deal about Torah! And I also learned a lot about partnering with someone who could have been wedded to his own wording or content, but instead accepted my input graciously and incorporated my suggestions.

In addition to our approach to the work, we modified our format and organization of the book several times. In the end we decided that the booklet format would allow us to make meaty yet "bite sized" volumes. Due to our determination to be helpful to the process and to each other, idea exchanges were fluid, cordial, even funny at times as our mutual enthusiasm for subject permeated our work.

We also needed to address how to write the words and names that often appeared in other publications in English but whose origins were Hebrew. I suggested that we could use this opportunity to share the original Hebrew names and words as part of the learning process, and as a way to connect to the characters and places in the Torah and Shaya agreed. We also agreed on writing a glossary so that people could easily translate from the Hebrew to the more familiar (in most cases) English. We hope using this approach will deepen the reader's experience.

We further hope that anyone who reads this book, whether tenuously connected to Judaism or looking for an engaging heartfelt approach to the faith, will be rewarded for his or her effort, and anyone who is simply interested in understanding the devotion of two very different Jews to this 3,000-year-old religion will find themselves intrigued and delighted.

We hope that this work helps communicate our enthusiasm for the Torah and how it can guide our lives in meaningful, good, and holy ways.

Shaya Cohen   Susan Quinn

GLOSSARY

Aharon	Aaron
Akeidoh	the binding of Isaac
Amorrah	Gomorrah
Avraham, Avram	Abraham
Beis HaMikdosh	Temple
Chavah	Eve
Chol	the beginning or natural state
Esav	Esau
Hashem	God
Hevel	Abel
Yosef	Joseph
Kayen	Cain
Korach	rebelled against Moses during the Exodus
Mishkan	Tabernacle
Mishnah	the first significant document that captured the Oral Law
Mitzvos	precepts and commandments from Hashem
Moshe	Moses
Rivkah	Rebecca
Sarai	Sara (before her name changed to Sarah)
S'dom	Sodom
Talmud	ancient Rabbinic writings composed of Mishnah and Gemara
Teshuvah	the process of repentance and growth
Tzaraat	a visible affliction that indicates a spiritual problem
Yaakov	Jacob
Yitzhak	Isaac

ACKNOWLEDGEMENTS

Building up to a work like this has taken many, many years.

I must thank my parents who, throughout my childhood, provided an environment where lively arguments about Big Questions were always welcome: where the substance of an argument mattered regardless of the identity of the arguer. I learned from them that, when hunting the truth, weak assertions are worse than useless. It is crucial to erect a strong and clear thesis, and then see how well it stands up to sustained assault. My mother helped me respect the power of intellect, while my father showed me how intellect and reason melt away when confronted by sheer force of will.

I wish to thank Yoram Hazony for first positing to me that it was possible for a person today to add to the *etz chayim* that is the Torah, in *midrashic* explication. Until that moment, as a fresh high school graduate in 1989, such a thing had never crossed my mind. An epiphany can be sparked by a single word. This one took a long time in germinating, but it made an indelible impression on me.

Akiva Ehrenfeld changed my Torah life in a similar way: he made me understand that not only is it possible for *a* person to add to our understanding of the Torah, but that the person in question could be yours truly. It happened on the day he said to me, "That is a really interesting idea!" It seems like such a simple thing to say. But it changed my life. The right word at the right time can change a person forever.

I was also greatly inspired by the work of

David Gelernter, who wrote a series of essays in *Commentary* magazine. Gelernter writes a great many things about a wide range of subjects. But those essays were not of this world. They shone with divine inspiration, every word delectably plucked and placed. I realize, as I read his words, that when we aim to understand Hashem, He helps us get where we are going.

It is one thing to have an idea. And entirely another to do something about it. And for this, I owe an eternal debt of gratitude to my *rebbe*, Rabbi Shaya Milikowsky. I do not, in this text, talk about how important it is to have a close and personal relationship with a *rav*, but that is in part because I am not able to explain just how much he has changed my life through his profoundly empathic and individualistic approach to Judaism. It was through Rabbi Milikowsky that I came to understand that every Jew has their own arc, their own unique relationship to Hashem, and that the answers to questions have to be understood in the context of the questioner. In other words, each person's relationship to the Torah, and to Hashem, is unique and personal.

And this work only started being written when Rabbi Milikowsky told me to start writing. He has guided me from the beginning, especially teaching me how to write positively.

Thanks to Rabbi Milikowsky, this work is not interested in quarreling, or drawing stark divisions between myself and others. Nor am I interested in labels and categories. We should be vigilant against using the Torah as a drunk uses a lamppost: for support, and not illumination.

I must also acknowledge a true giant in the Torah world, a man who is singularly the most brilliant and creative Torah mind I have ever met, and the inspirer of many of the ideas contained herein: Simcha Baer. Rabbi Baer has sometimes been a muse, and sometimes a collaborator. He is an exemplar of what the human mind, infused with *ruach hakodesh*, can achieve. I wish that I could grasp all that he has to share!

My sons Toyam, Asher, Kalev and Shai have also been very important collaborators in this work. I bounce ideas off of them all the time, and they have not only acted as sounding boards, but also as originators of some truly beautiful *chiddushim* of their own. The greatest blessing a father can have is to be surpassed by his children, and I pray, with all my heart, that each of my children, in their own unique way, outshines me.

I also acknowledge, with thanks and praise, the influence of Jonathan Sacks. His writing is poetry itself, and his ideas have often provided a jumping-off point for my own. Whether we agree or disagree, his weekly words on Torah have been a source of inspiration to me.

I must thank, on bended knee, my wife

Nechama, the very embodiment of an *ezer knegdo*. Words cannot express my love and appreciation and devotion to the woman who has inspired me, and shown me both the enormous gap between a man and his spouse (in heaven and on earth)—and to revel in the surpassing beauty that is produced in the bridging of that gap.

1 WHAT DOES IT MEAN TO BE A JEW?

Do you ever wonder why Western Civilization—the birthplace of capitalism, industrialism and modern medicine—is one of the most advanced civilizations in the world for technology and innovation? How persecuted religious people who fled England happened to be the people who brought their ideas for innovation and risk-taking to the United States, and how the seeds they planted in the U.S. have supported our becoming the world's leader almost since our inception? There are reasons for these accomplishments.

This country was founded by people who wanted to escape oppression and strike out on their own for religious freedom. From the start, we were guided by principles that were used to create a civilization that was entirely new. Those principles promoted the ideas of religious freedom (and with it, tolerance), independence and creativity. We believed from the start in possibilities and opportunity. The Founders crafted our government based on ancient texts, but particularly on Judeo-Christian principles and the Jewish Bible—the same Bible that teaches us that we are free agents with divine spirits, created in the image of Hashem. And because Hashem creates, we know that we have the power to create, and are commanded to be creative beings.

If you are reading this book, the idea of creation speaks to you specifically and to your own life. That's why this book is about you.

You have decided, for your own reasons, to take the journey of a lifetime. You may be viewing it with trepidation, excitement and curiosity, but you've decided to at least look into the life-changing potential that this trip offers.

The personalities in the Torah are a mixed bunch: they are heroes and villains; they are generous and greedy; they are risk-takers and reluctant to join in. At first, you may think you know them, but you will discover that they have much more depth and complexity than you ever imagined. You will realize that they are not strangers at all, but that you are connected to each and every one of them in some way.

The guidebook we will use on this expedition is thousands of years old and has stood the test of time. It will provide you with rules to live by, profound spiritual inspiration, and opportunities for growth. The degree to which you decide to dive in to this experience will be up to you.

By now, you likely realize that I am describing Torah and the Jewish people. Whether you are an observant Jew, a fallen-away Jew, a skeptical Jew or a

Jew hungry for a deeply spiritual life, you have come to the right place.

For some, Judaism is something of a tribal faith, joined by accident of birth or a mutual attraction to bagels and lox (!) For others, Judaism is far more rigorous and demanding. Nevertheless, this book contains much that will surprise every reader, and all Jews are welcome here. Questions and curiosity are encouraged, as we explore what it all means.

We will look at the query, "What does it mean to be a Jew?" through a number of stops on our journey: asking questions; being part of something bigger; timeless stories; our role in improving the world; and what it means to be holy.

2 ASKING QUESTIONS, CHALLENGING HASHEM

Some religious traditions discourage their faithful from asking questions. Not only does Judaism encourage us to ask questions, but we even see our forefathers arguing with Hashem!

Since we are Jews, it is the critics, and not the lazy, who dominate the conversation. Nobody wants to think of themselves as being in the wrong, or as being merely weak: it is much "stronger" to make a principled argument.

And so, for the critics, it is not enough to merely say that we should follow the laws of keeping kosher for the reason given by so many devout Jews, "because the Torah and our Sages say so." After all, we are a thinking people, and thinking leads to *critical*

5

thinking. And, arguments like "Hashem says so" aside, it seemingly makes no sense that we are allowed to eat a grasshopper, but not a hare; a cow, but not a pig.

As a result, Jews throughout time have followed the Torah by picking and choosing their commandments, or deciding not to follow the Torah at all. Korach, who rebelled against Moshe's leadership, made these arguments, as did Jesus' followers, and so have thousands of years of very intelligent critics and independent thinkers up to the present day. So today's critics are in very good company.

The critics are not necessarily wrong. At least, they are not wrong to ask. We are meant to ask questions. Following in the footsteps of our forefathers, we Jews are meant to ask questions—and demand answers—not only of ourselves but also of Hashem Himself. Being Jewish means more than just being carried along by the social and traditional forces that envelop and propel us. It means choosing one's own path in life. And Jews of every stripe should be as self-aware of their choices as possible. That means asking the Big Questions, even arguing with Hashem.

Unfortunately, our modern world is so very capable and technologically advanced that it is hard to credit the possibility, or even the probability, that most people, most of the time, remain as rudimentary in their thinking as were our pagan ancestors. I would go so far as to suggest that the vast majority of people are, when it comes to making sense of the world, as simple-minded as those island primitives who worshipped American soldiers in World War II because they came bearing goodies.

It is well worth mentioning that this dichotomy between a world enslaved to primitive thinking and a world in which mankind tries to aspire to greater meaning and accomplishments is by no means a modern creation. This dichotomy is at the heart of the Exodus from Egypt.

Egypt was the home of nature-worship. Its idols were the things these ancient scientists could touch and feel – the sun, the Nile... every physical force was its own deity in some way or another. All mankind had to do was to live in harmony with nature, and life would be predictable and safe. It would also, of course, be as meaningful as the lives of any animal that lives in harmony with nature. Which is to say, entirely without any meaning at all.

Torah Judaism was so enormously different in qualitative ways than other religions that even its adherents had (and still do have!) a hard time wrapping their heads around what it all means. Judaism has no shortage of laws or rules or regulations – but they are all either practical (as in matters of society and law), or symbolic, to show us how to connect with Hashem and each other, to create holiness. Instead of living in harmony with nature, Hashem, in the Ten Plagues, shows His superiority over the simple-minded ancient Egyptian scientist who sees only Nature, and not its creator, as the measurable forces in this world. The Torah keeps telling us, from beginning to end, that we have free will: there is no destiny unless we believe it to be there. Nature is as false and uncaring a god as were those American wartime logistics personnel who brought food into Pacific islands and created Cargo Cults.

What primitive thinkers of every kind fail to understand in their guts is that externalizing our understanding of the world to Mother Earth or Fate or Destiny or superheroes or the Nanny State is equivalent to outsourcing our own lives. When we do that, we are not really alive, and our lives are no more valuable, in the scheme of things, than the lives of any animals on this planet. Everything that lives will die; that is unavoidable. The question is whether or not we make our lives matter: whether we live by the 6 days of physical creation (Egypt), or the 7 days of creation that includes our Creator (static monotheism), or the 8 days that include mankind's contributions to the world, our partnership with Hashem in improving the world around us.

Even while Hashem expects us to make our own contributions, He allows us to find our own path and create our own story. One might think, for example, that a relationship with Hashem is accessible only to great scholars, to the holiest of people. The Torah tells us otherwise! Bilaam was an idol worshipper, and he was given the gift of prophecy. Avraham's first connection to Hashem, according to the simplest meaning of the text, was that Hashem saying to him, "*Lech Lecha*"—Go Out. There is no indication that Avraham was at that moment, a particularly righteous man.

Taken to its absolute extreme: a man whose parentage was unclear, who dressed as an Egyptian, and who married a non-Jewish woman while living away from any Jewish community was given the opportunity to speak with Hashem at the burning bush—and this man, Moshe, became the conduit for the entire Torah and our greatest leader. But at that first moment at the *sneh*, he was "just" someone who saw something off the beaten path – and investigated it.

Every person has his or her own story. We are not meant to be like everyone else--or even any other single person! These opportunities to connect with Hashem and each other are individualized and unique. The common thread is that the Torah shows us the way, by explaining what it all means, helping us discern the moral path. But once a person makes a decision, for good or ill, the Torah moves on. While the text is strict, we can (and do) choose to be lenient, with no conflict. What is done is done. Peculiarly for a nation that is so old, we do not dwell on the past. We prefer, instead, to always focus on what we can or should do *next*. For as long as there is life, there is an opportunity to do good.

As we work to clarify our path and continue to ask questions, we debate within ourselves and with Hashem. When Hashem decided to destroy S'dom, and told Avraham his plans, Avraham not only argued with him, but tried to negotiate with him. (You probably know that Hashem won that argument, though Avraham certainly gained ground.) When Hashem asked Moshe to lead the Jewish people from Egypt, Moshe refused to do it, pleading a speech defect; Moshe said Hashem should choose someone else to do the job. Finally Hashem became angry and told Moshe that his brother, Aharon (whom Moshe loved) would speak on Moshe's behalf. At Mt. Sinai, after the Jewish people built the golden calf, Hashem was prepared to destroy them, but Moshe argued with Him and convinced Him not to kill the people.

Hashem states going forward: *Before your entire*

people I shall make distinctions [wonders]. Except that the Hebrew is not "before," or *lifnei*: it is *neged*, which means "opposed." This verse does not only say that Hashem will make wonders in our future, but it says that these wonders will come about as a result of *conflict* between Hashem and us. The immediate parallel text is the creation of Chavah, Eve: she is created as a helpmate to oppose Adam. Man needs a wife who helps and opposes, testing, questioning, and pushing. There is not always domestic bliss in the Torah. Indeed, domestic bliss might even be a sign of a dysfunctional relationship!

The Torah tells us that in the wake of the sin with the golden calf, Hashem recognized that the Jewish people were not going to take Hashem's laws, behave perfectly, and live happily ever after. Hashem pushes us, and we push back. Hashem throws challenges in our path, and we pray, and question, and sometimes even rage at Him. We rebel and go off the path: as a nation we never fully break loose, and yet we do not fully submit to His will either.

The verse ends with, ". . . *and the entire people among whom you are will see the work of Hashem.*" This verse cannot apply to our time in the wilderness, of course, for the Jews were not living among other nations. This prophetic verse is about the thousands of years of Jewish exile, and of Jewish existence today among the nations of the world. It is the Jewish people who are the miracles and wonders that show Hashem's greatness—not because we are perfect servants of the Creator of the world, but because we are a difficult and obstinate people, always questioning and pushing back, and even sinning. Marx and Freud may have been self-hating Jews, but these examples only prove the rule, as we can now translate the verse: "*In opposition to your entire people, I will make wonders.*" A very great many of the Jews who changed the world were not obedient servants of Hashem, but they were Jews nonetheless. Even rebellious Jews, in opposition to

Hashem, could and did create wonders.

The referenced verse turns the utopian vision of a "happily ever after" on its head: great things will come about as the **direct result of** the creative tension, the wrestling match, between Hashem and His people. This verse is forecasting that the Jewish people will sin. Hashem, after the destruction of the first tablets at Mt. Sinai, now accepts this ingrained facet of the Jewish personality. And He will oppose us, and quarrel with us. The product of this oppositional engagement will be wonders that will make the Exodus from Egypt pale in comparison. Jews and Hashem will tussle throughout history, and **as a result of that continued opposition, we produce great miracles—in every creative endeavor, including science, technology, politics and human relationships.**

Whether through partnership with Hashem or in opposition to Him, we are making choices, exercising our free will. Our decisions, of course, are often made in ignorance – people make choices for all kinds of reasons that may not be rational or well-informed. Nevertheless, as Jews, it seems reasonable that before we choose *not* to follow Hashem's suggestion, that we at least familiarize ourselves with the choices in the first place. Free will without knowledge is little more than instinct, after all. Even Adam and Chavah heard the arguments of the snake before deciding to eat the forbidden fruit! And what they heard led them to *choose* to disobey Hashem's command!

Hashem told Adam and Chavah not to eat from the Tree of the Knowledge of Good and Evil. They knew that with the fruit came knowledge and a divine power to create new things. Before they ate the fruit, Adam had named the animals. But once Chavah arrived, the pair of them stopped creating at all! And among the many revealed dualisms would be Good and Evil, and endless decisions between which to choose. In other words, the one choice that they made led all of humanity into a world where we are confronted with decisions every waking moment.

Eating from the fruit triggered the entry of Adam and Chavah into the world we inhabit today. It is a pre-existing condition of our existence that we can— and must—make choices.

Just as Adam and Chavah had to make a choice, when Hashem told the Jewish people to leave Egypt, so they were faced with a simple decision: do we stay or do we go? The midrash tells us that only a minority of Jews chose to leave. The rest stayed in Egypt. Just as Adam and Chavah *could* have done, the Jews remaining in Egypt chose the path of least resistance, the path where they would no longer have to make choices at all.

The decision for Adam and Chavah was not merely whether they should pursue a new world— they were well aware that Hashem had told them *not* to eat the fruit. The question was whether to listen to Hashem or not. They chose to rebel. Many generations later, the Jewish people in Egypt were faced with the very same choice, and the actions of the minority who left were a corrective act, a *tikkun,* for the choice of Adam and Chavah, because the Jews who left Egypt chose to follow Hashem's command, while Adam and Chavah did not.

To some extent, Judaism is about being willing to ask questions – and being willing to find different answers than other people. There is no more a universal "right answer" to a deeply personal question than there is a universally ideal husband or wife. But the key to finding good answers is to keep asking questions!

It is the asking, the yearning to know and understand deeply, that is at the heart of each thinking Jew.

All of these stories, through events and people, relate great truths: that we can make choices between good and evil; how we can connect spiritually with

Hashem; whether we listen to Hashem; and the power of the choices we make in life, as well as many other lessons I haven't discussed here. So the stories are not just stories: they are guidelines, signposts, examples and at the deepest level, spiritual messages for us to integrate into our lives and assist us in developing our understanding of what it means to be a Jew and what our role is in the world.

So whatever your beliefs and attitudes about Judaism, Hashem expects us, wants us, to interact with Him. Our forefathers challenged Him, and we, in our prayer, can also call out to him in our questioning, in our sorrow, in our confusion. Practicing Jews who study Torah and much of the Written and Oral Torah ask and answer (with many options to choose from) about the reasons behind the commandments and the actions of the people in the Torah. For now, it is an opportunity for you to put aside judgments, criticisms and disappointments, of Judaism and yourself, and present those questions that you wish to be answered.

And if you persevere and listen closely, answers will come to you.

3 BEING PART OF SOMETHING BIGGER

It's interesting that early on, our forefathers seemed to want to live together, but none of them actually did.[1] And there was no complaint; they did not seem unhappy, nor consider it untoward that once children discovered their independence—when Avraham discovered Hashem, when Yitzchak survived the Akeidoh (Avraham's attempt to sacrifice him), and when Yaakov left Israel, knowing he might never see his father again, they all acted willingly.

But this practice changed with Yaakov. While he may not have been interested in living with his parents, Yaakov certainly wanted to live with his children, and his children reciprocated. By Yaakov's sunset years, the family united in one place. Once

Yaakov and his sons developed these types of relationships, they were ready to grow into a nation.

I think that there is a progression of these relationships within Genesis that mirrors the book as a whole: by the end of the book, the older generation is clearly *investing* their own selves and even extending the relationships that they have with Hashem, *with* the younger generation. Women do it first, but the men get there a generation later – and we know children need both parents to be involved.

When fathers started spiritually investing in their children, it became possible for people to move forward, from generation to generation. ***Building upon the previous generation is the most essential building block for a changing civilization – and more than this, the essential ingredient for historical progression.***[2]

From this point on, the pattern is set, and the

Jewish nation can gestate in Egypt and be born in the splitting of the waters of the Red Sea. All of the trends that advanced in Genesis have reached a level of maturity wherein it is possible to grow and nurture a nation, a nation ready to institutionalize these lessons and grow lasting and binding relationships with each other and with Hashem. They needed to see themselves as the nation of Israel, a nation of love, a nation where the fathers and sons loved one another, and wanted to be near each other, and where the people developed bonds across families, around the world, and to Hashem.

Being part of something bigger is more than connecting between people: it also means connecting with ourselves, with our divinely-gifted souls. We are supposed to be driven by our spiritual hunger, our attraction to energy in all its forms.[3]

In addition, we are called to take responsibility for our lives, not be victims of it. For instance, in the story of Yaakov and Esav, Yaakov convinced Esav to sell his birthright to Yaakov in exchange for a bowl of soup. Even later, Yaakov convinced their father, Yitzchak, that he was Esav (due to his father's poor eyesight) and Yitzchak gave Yaakov a special blessing. Later, when Esav realized the loss he had brought on himself, he saw himself as a victim, and cried out to his father; at that moment he changes from the man of action to the man who has been wronged, who wallows in the injustice of it all. Esav becomes passive, resentfully complaining that his brother had done him wrong. Oblivious to the bigger picture, Esav never tries to reconnect with Hashem, and even his half-steps to reconcile with his father (by taking on a non-Canaanite wife) do not manage to close the gap. Esav has assimilated with the peoples around him. He becomes a victim in his own mind, to avoid responsibility for his own actions, and conceding to the circumstances in which he finds himself.

In the eyes of his father, Esav has been transformed. *Judaism must be carried by those who are proactive, who boldly do what they think is right – even when they might well be wrong!* And that person was Yaakov, who seized the moment, even if he did it in error. Esav, by contrast, quit. And then he whined about it.

Esav's statement "he took away my birthright; and, behold, now he hath taken away my blessing," also tells Yitzchak something very important indeed: that Yaakov craves a relationship not only with his father, but has, for years, craved that relationship with Hashem! This story tells us that we must be forthright and responsible in our relationships with each other, as well as in pursuing our relationship with Hashem.

Since we are made from Hashem's own spirit, you might think we would easily recognize our potential for having a relationship with Him; unfortunately, mankind seems bent on forgetting it or is blissfully unaware of it. Across the world most people don't realize their connection to Hashem; even in the West, secularists insist on thinking of man as merely another animal. We have a soul, but it is only active if and when we seek it.

As the Torah relates, before Avraham, mankind kept forgetting that Hashem even existed. The Jewish tribe managed to keep a flame alight, but it failed to convert or otherwise improve the rest of the world. The Torah tells us of a progression – a necessary one – to a nation capable of serving as a light unto the rest of the nations. And that progression came with the understanding and acceptance of the idea that Hashem lives AMONG the Jewish people – the ever-present reminder of the divine presence that people somehow lose track of in their everyday lives. A simple but profound way to understand Hashem living among us is with the building of the *sukkah*.

A *sukkah* is a temporary hut, built for an eight-day

festival that comes after Yom Kippur. A sukkah is, itself, by definition a temporary structure, and so it is constructed quite poorly. Sukkahs are also highly individualistic. They come in a vast range of shapes and sizes, with seemingly-infinite customization, all within the letter and spirit of the Law. In this, sukkahs reflect the personal preferences and aesthetics of their makers. Each family makes its own sukkah, as a proxy for the way in which we choose to beautify the commandment and our relationship with Hashem.

And yet, these buildings are fragile. They cannot stand up to nature, or much (if any) external abuse, because (as required by Jewish Law) their roofs can offer little or no integral resistance to the forces around them. Yet we can look up through those roofs and invite Hashem to be present with us in our humble abodes.

So, too, the Jewish people can be seen as fragile. Outside of Israel, Jews have not effectively defended themselves in thousands of years. We seemingly have no real resistance to anti-Semitism, the forces of assimilation, the allures of our host countries and cultures. And still, every year, we, like our sukkahs, stand up once again. We keep coming back.

When we rely on "buildings," we decay. When we connect with living and dynamic ideas, then we remain capable of creative thought and growth. Judaism has certainly changed and adapted, but it has always sought to do so while remaining within the letter of the law. Like our sukkahs, we certainly bend and flex and sometimes blow completely over. But we'll keep rebuilding our sukkahs every year, once again demonstrating our belief that it is each person's personal connection with Hashem, as fragile and mortal as it is, that matters above all. The hardiest institutions are not made of bricks-and-mortar; they are made of our constantly renewed love and service.

Once we move forward and realize we can take charge of our lives and are free to relate to Hashem, the formal way Hashem reminds us of His presence within the Jewish people, within the world, and within each soul, is the Tabernacle, the Mishkan, that we are commanded to make. The Mishkan exists to not only remind us that Hashem is there, but also to serve as a reminder of why WE are here! The Mishkan became a key to accessing and using our divinely-inspired souls for good.

Like the five curtains on each side of the Mishkan, each curtain had a breadth of four amos: the same dimension as one human being! So we know where Hashem resides today: within the four corners of those who seek to have a relationship with Him. Hashem is inside us, as and when we choose to connect with Him. And the awareness of Hashem within us is a common bond that we share with every other Jew.

In spite of the call to invite Hashem into our lives, and our opportunities to do so, we become distracted by the dilemmas of our everyday lives. We complain—a lot. Letting life happen *to* you is something people who suffer silently do quite well. If you believe in the fates or the stars or other beyond-our-control influences that dictate our lives, then complaining serves no function whatsoever. This goes quite some distance toward explaining why billions of people in places like India and China and Africa, whose faith is in fate, quietly accept their lots in life. For a Jew, apathy is worse than kvetching.

But complaining may be a necessary step forward in growing up – it is a rejection of the status quo, and a desire to improve one's lot in life. In other words, *not* being happy with the cards that have been dealt you is the first step in learning how to take charge of your own life.

Being part of something bigger does not mean

that we are meant to be like ants in a colony; to the contrary, Judaism is all about individuality. Every person has his or her own story. We are not meant to be like everyone else - or even any other single person! These opportunities to connect with Hashem and each other are personal and unique. The common thread for Jews is that the Torah shows us the way, by explaining what it all means and by helping us discern the moral path.

4 TIMELESS STORIES

We began this booklet with the comment, "This book is about you." We made this statement because the stories in Torah show us people who are heroic, determined, and courageous—in other words they are in some ways greater than each of us individually, but they are also *just like us*: they desire love, justice, opportunities, success, and perhaps most importantly, want a relationship with Hashem.

When we first read the stories of Torah, it's easy to take them at face value, perhaps unintentionally ignoring or skimming over the reasons behind the actions the characters take in those stories. We may not have the tools to read beyond the obvious, to meditate on their meaning or determine the underlying messages.

Much is lost when we assume we understand Torah only from within our modern context. We are limited by sometimes reading the Torah as if it were a lightweight work to be skimmed cursorily. But if we are willing to take a little more time, we can dive deeper. Because these stories and their players have much to teach us about what it means to be a Jew.

Let's take an example of diving deeper, of where the "obvious" answers are either more complex or indeed, simply wrong: **Exodus from Egypt.**

The story of the enslavement of the Jewish people in Egypt is a fundamental story of slavery and freedom in Judaism. In many ways, this story has much more to teach us than these simple events; it tells us ways that Hashem calls us to live our lives, what it means to be free and creative human beings. We annually relive the Exodus from Egypt, family by family, year after year – and we have been doing it for well over 3,000 years! Pesach is the annual touchstone for the Jewish people, the single most observed festival among Jews today.

When we study the story of the 400 years in Egypt, we realize the Jews had become accustomed to much of the Egyptian culture. They were surrounded by idol worship, imbued with the ideas of fatalism and victimization, believing that they had no choice but to live within the Egyptian culture as slaves. So when Hashem commanded them to leave Egypt, even accepting this choice seemed impossible. Egypt had accustomed them to accepting life as it was, not to expanding their world and obeying the words of Hashem. Whether the Jews chose to stay or leave, they realized the consequences of their choices: they were *free to choose*.

And yet, as my sons argued during the Passover seder, it seems that the **Jewish people, for over 3000 years, have been getting a basic fact about our slavery in Egypt wrong.** And we have done it because, although Jews are incredible change agents everywhere we go, we fall short when it comes to changing ourselves, and especially our victimhood culture.

Who enslaved the Jews? It is a simple, patently foolish question. The Egyptians did, *of course*. Everyone knows that! The Haggadah tells us so. We were innocent victims, oppressed by a stronger nation that believed that Might Makes Right.

But my sons pointed out that this "obvious" answer is entirely unsupported by the Torah itself. Not only does it lack support, but the Torah gives us another explanation entirely. Nowhere does it say that the Egyptians enslaved the Jews. Sure, they assigned us taskmasters, ramped up the demands, and tried to kill our newborns. **But the Egyptians did <u>not</u> enslave us in the first place.** Here's the punchline:

The Jews enslaved themselves.

We study the story of Yosef and his brothers in Egypt After their father, Yaakov, died, the brothers were panicked, and they begged for Yosef's forgiveness. But they also went one step too far:

"[Yosef's brothers] went and fell down before his face,

and they said "Behold we are your servants."[4] [The Hebrew word for "servant" and "slave" are identical.]

The Jewish people enslaved **themselves** to the senior administrator of the kingdom of Egypt. And they did so for reasons that are entirely familiar to frustrated modern libertarians: fearful in the face of volatile uncertainty, they opted to restrain their freedoms in exchange for a predictable future.

What does Yosef say in response? He does **not** say "On the contrary! You are free men!" He does not avow the declaration in any way. Instead, his response is the same as that of every well-meaning government employee ever since:

"Have no fear… I will sustain you and your little ones."[5]

In other words, Yosef could be trusted, because he was an angel. And we don't need to worry about our freedoms when we are governed by angels. Alas, as James Madison put it, "If angels were to govern men, [no] controls on government would be necessary."

36

Yosef may have been a wonderful man; but the enslavement and welfare dependence of the Jewish people, once the first step down that slippery slope had been taken, had an almost-unavoidable conclusion: the complete elimination of the Jewish people. The road to serfdom is the easy path and it is almost always a one-way trip. Only direct divine intervention saved us just before the end.

But even though Hashem delivered us from Egypt, we never quite grew out of the classic Jewish slave-and-ghetto mentality. Like Yosef's brothers, we are too quick to shed the robes of freedom when offered the chance to wallow in perpetual victimhood, too quick to prefer dependable servitude over unpredictable--risky--freedom. By surrendering ourselves to Yosef, we opened the door to walking away from independence and free will, and we became capable only of biological multiplication and hard labor for a capricious overlord.

But we must never forget: **we did this to ourselves**.

And while Hashem took us out of Egypt, something for which there is no limit to the gratitude we should show, He did not do it just because He wanted us to be grateful: He did it so that we could make our lives productive and creative, to partner with Hashem, to ignite and spread holiness throughout the world.

And we work hard at it, handicapped because too rarely do we remember that we have to also heal *ourselves*, to realize that we are almost always our own worst enemies. External threats to the Jewish people, in Egypt and throughout time, are rarely diseases in their own right: they are symptoms of our own cowardice, unwillingness to tackle the flaws in ourselves and in the world for which we were given responsibility.

In order to grow, to become better and more complete people, we have to conquer our fears. In order to spread freedom, we need people to seek bravery, to eschew "safety." We must stop blaming other people, and playing the Victim Identity Game. In order to grow relationships and holiness with mankind and with

Hashem, we need to confront the terrifying insecurities that define our human existence.

We can learn other lessons from that time of exile. In one sense, this has been about internal development: maybe – just maybe – Hashem exiled us from our land so that we would be forced to grow. And grow we have! The number of texts that Jews produced (and preserved) from before the destruction of the Temple was a very, very small fraction (much less than 1%) of the creative work that has been produced since then, in the gigabytes and gigabytes of Jewish texts on law and thought.

And our growth has come in connection with others: Judaism "cast upon the waters" may have achieved far more than we could have ever done had we remained in one country, in one environment. Jewish contributions to innovation and creativity in every manner of human endeavor speaks for itself, but it is more than just, "Did you know that a Jewish person invented X?"

Jews do not seek to convert others to Judaism, but merely to inspire other people to be creative and productive in their own ways. Leadership is good, but partnership is good, too. So is merely identifying and applauding all the good things that others do; showing appreciation goes a long way toward overcoming the natural envies and fears that make it harder for people to take their own risks.

That connection can be (and usually *should be*) through personal connections, through conversations. In addition to the commandments and the testimonies and the statutes, we Jews are always enjoined to push forward – to engage with each other and with Hashem and with the world around us. And we must always seek to create positive things, things that, like light itself, had never existed before. The Torah is commanding us to be *imitatio dei*, to imitate our Creator by creating in turn, and connecting with the world.

Perhaps Jews are out here in the world because one cannot be "a light unto the nations" from faraway shores; we need to constantly interact and work with everyone, to help people find their own productive ways to contribute to the world around them: "what is right and good in the eyes of the Lord."

Just like the preservation of freedom, conquest over fear is a never-ending battle. The shared reward is the sweetest thing of all: satisfaction that we have not squandered the opportunities that lie before us, that we have lived our lives to the fullest.

That is what the Exodus from Egypt has to teach us: the lessons go far beyond the obvious.

Similarly, critics of the Torah often wonder about a Hashem who sometimes commands the obliteration of an entire people, or even directly causes the destruction of a city. Here is one of the most famous examples – and why it matters: **S'dom and Amorrah (Sodom and Gamorah).**

The cities of S'dom and Amorrah were not hostile to guests as a matter of custom: they *institutionalized* the practice, making it illegal for anyone to care for a stranger. While this institutionalization may have been a reaction to Avraham's hospitality to strangers, it also clearly showed that the society of S'dom had dug in its heels. S'dom was not destroyed just because it was wicked: it was destroyed because it signaled its complete and utter unwillingness to even consider spiritual growth. In other words, once S'dom sealed its wickedness into law, the divine logic applied to them as it had at both Babel and the Flood (and years later with Nineveh), and there was no longer any reason for the city to continue to exist. It was incapable of producing goodness then or in the future.

So when Avraham pleaded for the city to be saved if there were at least ten righteous men in the city, he made a very specific argument: that even institutional evil could be overcome if there are enough good people. And Hashem even agreed with Avraham's principal argument, so the question was simpler: how many people does it take to fix a society?

When a society absolutely refused to improve itself, as S'dom did, it would only take ten good people to have a chance to redeem it. But Avraham was not born into such a world. His world was one in which there was plenty of evil, but it was not eternally preserved in the laws of societies. In a society that is organized along evil lines, it took ten men for there to be any hope of reform. But in a world where most people just did what was right in their own eyes, acting with simple selfishness, then a single holy couple, such as Avraham and Sarah, could be (and clearly were) a light unto the nations, but were unable to save S'dom.

The lesson of S'dom came from a time when Hashem directly intervened in the world – a time when Avraham represented one family in the entire world. But after the Torah was given, the responsibility was handed to the Jewish people: we, as Hashem's only emissaries in this world, are directly responsible for combating evil.

How are we doing at selecting the good, at transforming bad societies and cultures to better ones? Ultimately this is not just a national or group effort: it always comes down to the individual.

When we look at our own society and its morality (or lack thereof), what do we see? What is our role in being a part of a society that is lacking morality? Do we yield to others' expectations? Do we try to maintain our own beliefs under the pressure to fit in with everyone else? And what are the ways we can take those steps? Some of those answers live in Torah, with Hashem and the Jewish people, as we try to fulfill our mission to bring light and justice to the world.

5 WHAT IT MEANS TO BE HOLY

We live in a world where the mundane is elevated: movie stars, fashion, glamour, ultimate fighting, race car driving, fancy cars, bigger houses and activities and experiences that set us apart from everyone else. The more daring, exciting and extreme a pursuit is, the more we admire it. And the more we want of it.

But at some point we realize the emptiness of those activities, how excitement is transient and true fulfillment is missing. And so we may not be able to name what we seek. But I—and the Torah—would call it holiness.

So what is holiness? Where does holiness fit into this world? And why do we desire it?

We can study the Tabernacle/Mishkan with its four

primary components: the Menorah, the Altar, the Show-bread, and the Ark: I believe they represent the four forms of holiness, of connection to Hashem:

Menorah: the menorah is a reminder to us of the burning bush (the first time holiness is named), as well as a reminder of light (of every kind – truth, revelation, clarity, etc.).

Altar: When sacrifices were offered to Hashem on the altar, man showed appreciation to Hashem, connecting heaven and earth. It was a way of elevating the physical into the spiritual plane, a holy act. The altar represents our role in improving the world by infusing everyday items and even trivial rituals with the transcendent and beautiful. Although the Sabbath is the completion of the world, the eighth day, Sunday, is the day that is "most holy" because it is the day when we roll up our sleeves and work, investing our own souls in our labors. The Sabbath day happened all by itself (and is never called "most holy" in the Torah). The work that *we* do to grow and preserve our relationship with Hashem is most beloved by Him, and is, like the meal offering, most holy in His eyes.

Showbread: The showbread represented the partnership between man and Hashem in sustaining life, and in creating new things, manifestations of the holy. The showbread is today showcased by man's incredible technological achievements.

Ark: The ark housed the tablets of the commandments, and it was crowned by male and female angels, showing the love between man and Hashem, as well as man and woman.

To the extent that we internalize these aspects of holiness (Light, Elevation, Partnership/Creation, and Love), *Hashem dwells within us.*

This view of the Tabernacle is that it, like the Torah, is not *descriptive*: it is *prescriptive*. We are to make our lives into lights, elevating ourselves and the world around us, and partnering with Hashem in creating new things to sustain life. If we do those things, then in the Holy-of-Holies, we are able to properly and fully love Hashem and each other.

In a sense the Ark (and the love embodied in it) is the *result* of a life devoted to the other aspects of holiness, in the same way that happiness is not something one achieves by directly seeking it, but is rather the byproduct of a life well spent. Judaism does not believe that there are shortcuts to this kind of love: one must actively choose to engage in spiritual growth in order to enjoy the resulting relationship with Hashem.

Holiness is antithetical to behaving like an animal. We are supposed to be connected to the earth and our animal passions, but we must be the master of these desires, not servile to them.

Holiness is not achieved easily, of course. For some holy acts, we must first separate from impurity, then undergo ritual purification, and then elevate the material toward the spiritual. All the laws of purity and impurity are there to help us achieve holiness.

Holiness is the combination of heaven and earth, and so we must be anchored in the waters of the earth, the *mikvah* (ritual bath), before we can elevate ourselves into the spiritual realm to seek holiness. This definition of holiness explains why Moshe had to remove his shoes at his encounter with Hashem: he would be stepping on holy ground, and so he was to connect with the earth in order to speak with Hashem.

But beyond the identification of that which is holy, **the Torah tells us of another sub-category of holy things: that which we call, using the spoken word, "holy."** Words are powerful—Hashem created the world with the spoken word alone. And we have the power to create holiness just by naming something as holy. We make things holy by declaring them to be holy, just as we declare the Shabbos holy when we make Kiddush (bless the wine) on Friday night. When we use our own bodies and souls to utter Hashem's name, then we can achieve tremendous heights of *k'dushoh* (holiness)—and we can just as easily profane His name.

What, then, does "unholy" mean? Unholy does not

mean defiled; instead the opposite of holy is the word in Hebrew, *chol*. This word is often defined as common or mundane, but it actually means *what came first*. Indeed, *chol* is the world the way Hashem made it, because nature is unfeeling, unthinking, and has its own rules. Nature, the way the world was created, is essentially a very large and complex automaton. And that automaton, a universe in which neither Hashem nor man is involved, does not fulfill any useful—holy—function, because it is incapable of improvement by itself. It merely *is*. And more than this: *chol* is the divided state, the way the world was created on the second day, the world we are meant to heal.

The Torah tells us that we are forbidden to make unnecessary separations in the world, since holiness comes from healing separations, not creating them. Rabbi Jonathan Sacks says, "For Jews, holiness lies not in the way the world is, but in the way it ought to be." The way the world is, is *chol*.

In order for *chol* to be improved, it needs the

addition of creativity, the application of Hashem's creative powers, expressed directly from Hashem—or even better, through a combination of Hashem and man.

So the above defines the absence of holiness, and how we can create holiness, as the co-existence of heaven and earth, of matter and energy, of man's body and soul and, importantly, man and woman. When we bring opposites together and still promote spirituality in that act, then we have created holiness on earth. This might explain why we say that Hashem Himself is holy!

On the face of it, Hashem is pure spirituality, the opposite of the limited and finite physical world. And this is so—except that we cannot ignore the power of perceptions. We call Hashem holy because in every respect we can perceive, Hashem is connected to us. We are the combinations of the dust, and of the life in which Hashem's spirit resides. And so we don't relate to Hashem in the purely ethereal realm that we cannot even imagine. We relate to Hashem on this earth, in his manifestations in the Mishkan and within human beings. Among all of these contributions, it is when we actively *choose* to find ways to elevate the physical into the spiritual plane, that we are fulfilling the purpose of our existence in the world.

6 IMPROVING THE WORLD

It isn't enough to be a good person or a good Jew. We are called to reach out to the world, to be a light among the nations, to be an example of the many ideas for which we stand. We have many ways to carry out these actions, whether they are with our friends and families, our communities, our country, or the world. To take these actions, we must continually be improving ourselves. The underlying question for all Jews throughout all of our history has always been whether we choose to grow or not. And by "grow," I mean taking our corporeal existence and aiming upward, always seeking to improve. Ideally, it is our mission to complete the creation of the world by healing the divisions that Hashem created when he separated the waters above and below.

In our own world, quite a few people think that the purpose of life is to be comfortable or stress-free. They aim to play things safe whenever possible. And for excitement, they seek experiences: sight-seeing, exotic cuisine, extramarital relationships, endless television, and even video games. These experiences are things that happen to us, but they do not necessarily change us, nor do they improve the world around us.

The things we accomplish with our lives are much, much more important than our experiences. A wedding is nice, but the experience of a *wedding* falls away in comparison to the accomplishment of a good *marriage*. So the one-time experiences of the Jewish people that we constantly remind ourselves of (the Exodus and receiving the Torah) are there to remind us of the accomplishments of Hashem, and to help to guide and direct our thoughts, words and deeds to His service.

Receiving the Torah at Sinai was a seminal moment, but the challenge to us is not remembering it (after all, we deliberately "lost" the location of the mountain), but bringing the Torah "back into our tents," incorporating the Torah into our lives. Receiving the Torah required little personal development, but using the Torah to *grow and improve ourselves and our world,* to make something of our opportunities, is the essence of our purpose in this life.

An example of embracing this mission to improve the world is near the end of Yom Kippur; we have made our peace with our fellow man, and we have made our peace with Hashem. United in prayer, we have also formed a union with all our fellow Jews. Late in the afternoon of Yom Kippur is when we begin to prepare to exit the national cocoon and connect with our individuality. At this time we have to recognize that it is not enough that we do mitzvahs and merely go through life by putting one foot in front of the other. We must consciously decide that we are going to bend our will towards serving the Creator by focusing all of our individual energies on our unique and holy potential to make the world a better place. It is the time for us to decide to harness our creative powers at both ends of the spectrum—from the choice of what we do with our reproductive talents to the choice of what we do with our mental talents—in our individually unique and beautiful service to Hashem.

"But," I hear you saying, "what about Hashem's will? Aren't things preordained?"

The Torah tells us they are not! Yet we have customs that suggest otherwise. Take, for example, the fast of Tisha B'Av that commemorates the destruction of both the First Temple and Second Temple in Jerusalem, which events occurred about 655 years apart, but on the same Hebrew calendar date. During those days, we mourn and many avoid engaging in normal levels of business. It seems like an inauspicious date, somehow a date that is fated to be bad luck for Jews.

Is that so? I ask this because I am reminded of the opinions of Rabbi Yochanan and Rav, that there is no mazal (luck) in Israel. Astrology, according to these opinions, is only for the non-Jewish world. We Jews are to look to Hashem for favor and blessings, and we do that by seeking and growing a relationship with our Creator, not by falling into astrology and superstition.

One might well counter, of course, that given the historical prevalence of tragedy on and around the Jewish date of the Ninth of Av, the time seems to be somehow unlucky, a time when Hashem has reserved His favor or otherwise hidden His face from us.

But here's the problem with the argument that Hashem caused all these events to happen: Hashem did not create the Ninth of Av: *we did*. It was the Jewish people, in the episode of the spies, who lost their nerve and lost their willingness to appreciate that our mission in this world is not just to be molly-coddled by Hashem in the wilderness, but to go out and bravely step up as Hashem's partners in this world. We are responsible for combating evil wherever we find it and promoting holiness at every opportunity. And when we failed to do it, we paid the price.

The Ninth of Av is a time to connect with our history, to understand what has gone so tragically wrong in our past, and what we can do to make the future brighter. We can focus on how best to improve and grow ourselves and the world around us. We are here to build and grow and soar, without fear that our goals might falter, without the fear that comes with accepting that there is only One Hashem and that He is not found in the forces of nature, and without ever forgetting that each person contains a divine spark, and is to be accorded love and respect on that basis alone.

Every tragedy in the world since then has been one that Hashem has allowed – not because Hashem is evil, but because He endowed all of humanity with free choice and the responsibility to make good choices Pestilence and destruction and evil in this world are *our* responsibility. The Ninth of Av, and the days preceding it, are not opportunities to wallow in loss, but to realize that we must do better, that we must right the wrongs of the past, by stepping up to our responsibilities as Hashem's partners in improving this world. We are not supposed to be passive actors; on the contrary!

Seen in this light, the fact that so many events happened on the same day is not meant to teach us that the beginning of the month of Av is a time of misfortune. Each tragedy is on the same date to reinforce, event by event, a lesson that we continue to stubbornly resist: we are not at liberty to shuck the immense responsibility riding on our shoulders. We are Hashem's people, and that means we must summon the courage to act like it: we must partner with Hashem to improve the world. Later I will discuss how you can apply your creative talents, even in the simplest ways, to improve the world.

The Torah tells us that we are not animals: we have free will, and we have (for a limited time only!) creative power from Hashem. Hashem created an imperfect world. But before He rested, He gave it the means to repair itself: mankind. We are all commanded to choose whether (and how) to improve nature: to bring light into darkness, to spiritually elevate the physical, to choose relationships and love.

The Torah gives us the canvas and the paints, and at every moment, the choices are open to us.

These ideas are not meant to be a comprehensive description of what it means to be a Jew, but they are some of the most important aspects of leading a Jewish life, and can provide much of life's meaning. We are not only part of a family, a community, a country: we are also part of a religion and tradition, whose roots are 3,000 years old. Not only can we practice the religion, but we are never separate from it. Even when we don't practice it or relate closely to Hashem, Hashem is always with us for us to experience, love and serve Him. He delights in our relationship with Him, even when we lose our way. And he's always available to re-connect actively with us.

Hashem is also our partner. He takes an interest in us, expects us to nurture the relationship so that He may reciprocate and connect with us. He welcomes, even expects our questions, anticipates our willfulness and confusion, and if we are patient and open, He will remind us that He is always nearby. Unlike other traditions where Hashem is distant, angry or to be feared, Hashem wants us to seek Him and be with Him. Whether we are celebrating or upset, Hashem can comfort and strengthen us, through good times and bad.

Through the stories of Torah, we can relate to and identify with the victories, hardships, disappointments, accomplishments, joy and sadness of our ancestors. We recognize ourselves in their life dilemmas, identify with their challenges and know that the mistakes they make mirror our own. When we dive deeply into the stories, we see that their life experiences are no different than our own: deceptions, conflicts, annoyances, and impatience; anxiety about responsibilities, outcomes and resolving dilemmas, joys, victories and love. We relate to the choices they must make; if we study, we see them in our everyday lives, because they are us—our friends, families and co-workers. We are a nation of many, yet inseparable.

Living in a mundane and secular world, we have the power, given to us by Hashem, to elevate the world and everything around us. We identify and name the sacred, bringing everything about our lives closer to Hashem, and He works with us to make that happen.

Opportunities to create holiness are all around us; we only need to open our eyes and take responsibility for naming the holy to be embraced by heaven.

And finally, we are here to improve the world. At first reading, that sounds like a huge task. But our everyday lives give us chances daily to make improvements, when we look around ourselves. Improving comes in many different forms: some are small, some are great, some are simple, and some are complex. But Hashem has asked us to continue His work of creation, to partner with Him with this significant ask.

All of these, and more, describe what it means to be a Jew.

7 LOVING YOUR NEIGHBOR

What is meant by the phrase, "Love your neighbor"? It seems like a simple statement, but in fact it tells us much about what Hashem expects us to embrace in ourselves, in others and in our relationship with Him.

We live in times where the extremes of self-love and self-hate seem to be battling with each other. Narcissism permeates social media, where people seem to think that the world centers on their lives in great detail. In contrast, the paradox also exists where people demonstrate their self-hate, even revulsion, for themselves; they deface their bodies, damage social norms, denigrate others and their ideas. They crave the attention of others, even though they send the message that they are unworthy of our consideration or respect.

In Judaism, Hashem demands we take a completely different direction in our lives. We are called to love ourselves, not in a narcissistic way, but in a generous way – as much as we can love others. Hashem believes we are worthy not only of our love for ourselves, but His love as well. As we learn to love ourselves, we open our worlds to others, and learn to appreciate their gifts, realizing that they, like us, are created in Hashem's image. They carry the divine spark within them, as do we.

Finally, when we learn to love ourselves, our friends, families and others in our universe, we are strengthened in our desire to love Hashem, too. We are, in fact, Hashem's servants and partners, challenged by the opportunities He opens for us, and also empowered to carry them out, with an even deeper love and commitment.

So this is an expression of how loving ourselves, our neighbor and Hashem are intertwined; how nurturing one relationship deepens our relationship within every case, and strengthens our resolve to be a devoted Jew, a good human being.

We explore love by looking at the many qualities that make up love, particularly with Loving our Neighbor (or all those who touch our lives), remembering that those actions are not separate from loving ourselves and Hashem. The qualities of love are generosity, give-and-take, responsibility, respect, gratitude, co-existence, happiness for others, fidelity, mercy and justice, joy, needing others, courage and the benefit of the doubt. We all possess these characteristics to different degrees and with various abilities to access them in our relationships with others. Still, focusing on each one of these deepens all of our relationships, suffuses our lives with joy and enriches our connections with all that we say and do.

8 GENEROSITY

We think that charity is easy to define: it is helping people by giving them things. At least, that is what we teach children. But this is a big mistake, even by the most well-meaning people. Charity is *not* "giving people things." Charity is about *helping people*. And there is a very simple proof:

> "And when you cut the harvest of your land, do not remove the edge of the field when you cut it, and do not gather the leftovers of your harvest. Leave them for the poor people and the strangers – I am Hashem."[6]

Simple enough, right? Command Ploni to leave his assets in the field, for Almoni to come along and help himself.

But if it is so simple that Ploni should help Almoni, why doesn't the Torah just say, "When you cut the harvest of your field, give 10% (or 20%) to the poor people and the strangers"?

The answer is simple enough: because it is not charitable to sap people of their own work, the pleasure and sense of accomplishment that we get for working for our own crust, even if it is from someone else's field.

The Mishnah (in Pei'ah) goes one step farther: *one who does not let the poor people gather the produce in the field but rather collects it himself and distributes it to them is **guilty of stealing from the poor**.*

Isn't that amazing? The realization that, many thousands of years ago, societal laws were passed down specifically to help people help each other – by raising each other up, by growing each person's sense of accomplishment and purpose. When we want to do real charity, we connect people with each other. Ploni's field is available; Almoni will come and work the corners. And both people become better for it. These charitable acts are loving acts.

9 GIVE-AND-TAKE

It might seem odd to try to "prove" the veracity of any religion over another, and merely measure those faiths by their fruits. But it can also be quite liberating to do so, because if we can accept that people often end up with the lives that they choose, then we can see religions (including the religious belief in an objective reality) through a utilitarian lens. And that lens is not merely about technological progress or new restaurants – it is also about morality.

The Torah tells us that each person is made in the image of Hashem, holding Hashem's divine spirit within us. That is an article of faith, surely. There is no proof of any such thing, and rationalists throughout history have argued that society would be better off if we did not allow cripples or ignoramuses to procreate or even, in some cases, to live. *Buck vs Bell*, the evil Supreme Court decision that permitted compulsory sterilization of the unfit, including the intellectually disabled "for the protection and health of the state," remains the law of the land. The fruits of such a morality can righteously be called "evil."

The problem we have, though, is that Hashem does not seem to value life either! After all, our world is populated by living things that will die. So instead of just understanding life as the ultimate good, there is an inherent tension between Hashem who supposedly loves us—and at the same time, allows us and our loved ones to suffer and die. The very same data about the world that leads to pagan religions can also lead us to worshipping the Jewish or Christian deity—or even death itself. After all death is at least as inevitable as life, and much easier to bring about. This is a central question within Judaism and Christianity that does not trouble those who simply make pace with living on the Great Wheel of life.

The Torah itself brings this tension out repeatedly. Hashem wants to destroy S'dom, but Avraham argues with Him – to save the city for the sake of those few who are righteous within it. Rather than seeing this as a problem with religion itself, the Torah is making it clear that it is both right and proper that man and Hashem see things from different perspectives: man must seek to preserve and grow life, because life represents the opportunity to do good.

Hashem, on the other hand, created death as well as life, and He barred the entrance to the Garden of Eden so as to keep man from becoming immortal: to Hashem, the life of man is not necessarily a good thing in itself. The only thing that matters to Hashem is what that life chooses to do, whether in fact we are actively seeking to improve the world, to keep the Great Wheel bumping along, and toward better places.

To me, the tension is not a bug: it is a feature. That tension keeps us on our toes, keeps us from being merely passive actors, placidly chewing our cuds as we go through life and await the inevitable date with the executioner. But it means that we are, in a real and tangible way, at odds with Hashem. The system is rigged, because we are both biologically and spiritually programmed to seek life, to seek to extend and preserve our own existences, even in the face of a world where death is the only guaranteed conclusion.

Hashem, on the other hand, loans out souls at the beginning of their lives, and then brings them back in again at the end. We live in a relationship of give-and-take with Hashem—He gives us life, and ultimately limits our time on this earth. Like planted seeds, the value of each life is in what they do while they are alive, even though the harvest is sure to come for all of us.

The story of Yosef and his brothers in Egypt demonstrate this idea of give and take. Early in his relationship with his brothers, Yosef proved to be immature, self-centered and emotionally distant from his brothers. As a result, even when they were re-united and Yosef took care of his brothers, they feared him and didn't trust him. Love was the missing ingredient. Without it, Yosef's "giving" led to distrust and resentment.

There is nothing wrong with being a "taker," as Yosef was for many years. We are all, in some ways, and at some times, takers. Indeed, I have argued that the Jewish version of slavery is nothing more or less than a patron/client relationship for when the client has fallen very far, and needs a mentor. Unequal relationships are just fine – but they require both the giver and the taker to respect the other, to invest in the relationship such that both sides benefit as a result.

Many devout Jews demonstrate this understanding

and are inspired by Avraham and Moshe, who argued and quarreled with Hashem when it came to how human life should be treated. We are in no hurry to reach that "game over" moment, and recognize that, as with any good marriage, there is considerable give and take between the spouses. Hashem's priorities are not our priorities, just as a husband and wife usually apply different priorities to everything from home décor to how one should spend leisure time. But the *conversation* that ensues in that disagreement is itself usually fruitful, and brings both parties together.

10 RESPONSIBILITY

No matter where we are on our path, we are always aware of the great responsibility we have for leading a life of virtue and for being willing to take risks. A Jew's life is not always an easy one; the Torah requires us to pursue a level of introspection about our lives, our faith, our relationships with others, and our connection to Hashem.

At the same time, we are empowered to not only take charge of our own lives, but to shine Hashem's light on the world. We do that through not only our faith, but through our actions and behaviors. The challenges will be many, but the rewards will be life-changing.

So I choose the scary path: the understanding of life and Hashem that gives me the most power – and the most responsibility for my own actions. It is a worldview that does not allow me to placate an impersonal deity with sacrifices or to submit to a personal deity by deciding that "whatever happens is all part of the Plan." Instead, Hashem is profoundly involved in every aspect of my life, and we talk several times a day. Sometimes I do all the talking. Sometimes I mostly listen. And sometimes we grapple with the issues together. Ultimately, though, when we are done, I am called to act in the world and to be responsible for the actions I take and the choices I make.

11 RESPECT

When we read the book of Genesis, we realize it is an arc, a progressive story showing changes from beginning to end, and is a treatise on respecting others.

Take for example the treatment of women. Before the flood, men "took" wives, whomever they chose[7]. Hashem immediately responded by limiting man's lifespan in an attempt to make men value women more. It was not enough, because even after the flood, women were primarily treated as chattel: Avram "took" Sarai. Sarai even "took" Hagar to present her to her husband. Both Avram and his son Yitzhak tolerated their wives being taken in turn by other men (such as Pharaoh) merely because those other men were more powerful.

The "might makes right" ethos of the ancient world clearly dominated.

This ended when Dinah was taken by Shechem – and her brothers stood up and put an end to rape from that point onward; there are no more examples in the Torah of a woman being taken by a man against her will. But even before then, Yaakov, unlike his fathers, did not "take" either of his wives or even his concubines; he was given them. Similarly, Yosef never takes his wife; he "comes in" to her. Moshe similarly did not "take" his wife – and the verses describing their marriage are followed by Hashem recalling the covenant, and starting the process that becomes the Exodus.[8] Marriage grows away from violence, and toward respect.

The power of women in the Torah similarly grows as the story unfolds. The women in Noach's time are not only chattel, but also have no speaking role.[9] Not so as the Torah progresses: Yaakov consults his wives before deciding to leave their father's house. And there is an even more striking contrast when one considers the midwives who, when summoned by Pharoah[10], lie to his face in order to save lives. These are women of courage and conviction, who accelerate the growth in the population, "and the people multiplied, and waxed very mighty"[11]. Moshe's wife, similarly is a woman of action and force, "Then Zipporah took a flint, and cut off the foreskin of her son, and cast it at his feet; and she said: 'Surely a bridegroom of blood art thou to me'"[12]. And when Miriam leads the women in song after the splitting of the sea, the journey is complete: women have a voice, a parallel and sometimes-independent role in the service and praise of Hashem. The Jewish people have risen to the level where they were able to merit the revelation at Sinai.

Families, of course, are often more than just the airing of concerns between husband and wife. Rabbi Jonathan Sacks has traced the arc of how brothers go from fratricide (Cain and Hevel) through every kind of competition and antipathy until Yosef's sons, the first brothers who are not jealous of the other – and then to Moshe and Aharon, the first brothers who are genuinely happy when the other succeeds.

But it is with the treatment of children that we see most starkly how far the world came from Noach until the Exodus. The Torah gives us an indication of how parents invested in their children, from a young age: by how the children were named.

Names before Yitzhak are given as if they were entirely passive: a child's name was "X." Yitzhak is named by his father, a father who cared a great deal about his son. But Yitzhak does not in turn name Yaakov and Esav – they are seemingly named by others, perhaps the midwives who called the children after their appearance at birth (Esav was hairy, and Yaakov was grasping at his brother's heel).

It is Leah who changes everything, going back to a

custom that had been lost since Adam, Chavah, and Seth: parents naming their children by way of reflecting their own relationship with Hashem. Chavah said: "And the man knew Chavah his wife; and she conceived and bore Cain, and said: 'I have gotten a man with the help of the Lord.'"[13], and then, with Seth, ". . . for Hashem hath appointed me another seed instead of Hevel; for Cain slew him."[14]

In other words, between Eve and Leah mankind had somehow forgotten that Hashem was a partner in the act of creating children. We no longer credited the ultimate Creator's role in our own creativity.

Women led the return to acknowledging Hashem's role: Chavah, not Adam, named their sons. Leah and Rachel both named their sons. The men (with the notable exception of Avraham naming Yitzhak) did not do so until Yaakov named his youngest, Benyamin. And then, just as with "taking" wives, it is as if a switch was flicked. Yosef names just as Leah and Eve had, in appreciation to Hashem:

> And Yosef called the name of the first-born
> Manasseh: 'for Hashem hath made me forget all
> my toil, and all my father's house.' And the name
> of the second called he Ephraim: 'for Hashem
> hath made me fruitful in the land of my
> affliction.'[15]

Fathers do not, of course, as a matter of biological necessity have to be very involved with their children. The Torah is telling us something else entirely: that when fathers connect with and relate to their children, and see their children in the context of the overall relationship between man and Hashem, that Hashem reciprocates, by in turn being more involved with *us*.

" [Moshe] called his name Gershom; for he said: 'I have been a stranger in a strange land.'"[16]is followed, only two verses later, by:

> And God heard their groaning, and God remembered his covenant with Avraham, with Yitzhak, and with Yaakov. And God saw the children of Israel, and God took cognizance of them.

The Torah is telling us, through the proximity of the verses, that there is a causal link between fathers loving their sons and Hashem in turn taking an interest in His children. The Exodus from Egypt follows.

Families are complex, and the Torah tells us about all of the various kinds of relationships. There is the nucleus, the relationship and respect between husband and wife, which is connected to whether women are seen as independent voices in their own right. There is the way in which brothers treat one another. There is the way that parents bring Hashem into the family, connecting their own biological creativity to Hashem's investment in us.

The Jewish people learned over time the importance of respect in developing loving relationships, and we follow their example today.

12 GRATITUDE

Of all the things that we can choose to accept or deny, gratitude is both the most optional, and also the single most important for our state of mind, the state of our families and our society.

Indeed, gratitude is probably even more important, at least in terms of concrete results, than whether or not someone believes in Hashem. After all, there are good and bad believers, just as there are good and bad atheists. But people who consistently choose to be grateful and appreciative of all that they are and all that they have, are invariably better people for it.

Still: gratitude remains nothing more or less than a choice, a state of mind. Even more than this, feeling grateful is something that we can induce entirely within our own thoughts; it is artificial. In other words: whether we are grateful or not is a choice that we make; it is proof that free will exists.

I choose to see all data through the prism of what Hashem wants from me. When a stray thought comes to me while I pray, I consider it as "the still, small voice," and I give it serious consideration. Whether it is sunny or it rains, whether I feel well or poorly, I choose to be grateful to Hashem for the opportunity to learn and to grow, and to accomplish.

Why, if I could choose another path, do I choose this one? In part, because my life is much more productive when I choose to be grateful for all that I have, for all that I and my loved ones have accomplished and achieved. I waste no energy stressing out about the things I cannot change; I do my part, with all my body and soul, and I am enormously grateful to know that Hashem will take care of the rest. He always has, and I pray that He always will.

I also choose to be grateful because it makes the world so much more wonderful. Nothing blesses a marriage like a husband and wife who, on an ongoing basis, express their gratitude for all that the other person does. Nothing makes a child feel more love than a parent who is grateful for their contributions to the family and all that it needs. Gratitude is a recursive loving loop, feeding back on itself. But in order to "work," gratitude must be personal.

The centerpiece of Jewish prayer is a silent prayer, *Amidah*, or *Shemoneh Esreh*. In it, we praise Hashem, and we pray for numerous good results. After each person has prayed silently, the prayer is repeated out loud by the leader, in every particular, except one. The section on gratitude is said by each person, on his or her own. It stands out. And the reason, our tradition tells us, is a simple and profound one: we can delegate our prayers. We can delegate our praise of Hashem, and our entreaties to Him. But the one thing we cannot ask another to do for us is to say "thank you." That is something all people must do for themselves.

Thus, gratitude forms the backbone of my faith, my marriage, my family, my business, and my life. I thank Hashem with every thinking breath. I see all data through this prism: if something that looks bad happens, I choose to see it, as hard as it can be, as an opportunity for something better to happen as a result, or as a spur for *me* to get smarter or see things differently. Rebuilding the world requires an appreciation for being alive, gratitude for the opportunity to work and act and live.

Gratitude is the foundation of everyone and everything I love.

13 CO-EXISTENCE

The Torah tells us[17] that when land is given over to a new owner to satisfy a debt, the Jubilee year comes into play. The underlying reason behind the Jubilee is that this same land must revert to the original owner every fifty years. Reversion of land did not make the poor rich or the rich poor, but it did remind everyone both that the land was ultimately a gift from Hashem, and that nobody can take their assets for granted. A rich man, for example, would have transferred his land rights to animals or storehouses for the Jubilee year--but unlike land, animals get sick, and storehouses can catch fire or the contents could rot or be stolen. A rich man who holds all his assets in non-land form for a year learns how to pray.

So the Jubilee was a way to make sure that everyone would periodically become "re-grounded" in an understanding that Hashem is in our world, and that we need that relationship. There is no real security in this world—and insecurity is what drives people into marriage, and brings people to connect with Hashem. But there is an exception.

> .. A house that is in the walled city passes permanently to its purchaser throughout his generations; it does not revert in the Jubilee.[18]

Why is there an exception for a walled city?

I suggest that there are two parts to the answer. The first part is that Hashem very much wants mankind to build and create. Our creations are always respected by Hashem—because our creations are, in a sense, extensions of Hashem's own power, funneled through our bodies and souls. We are here to improve upon the natural world, and providing an exception to the Jubilee would guarantee that people, seeking their self-interest, would build walled cities.

But the exception is not given for a walled home, no matter how impressive or expansive! No: the only property that does not revert is property inside a *walled city*. And a city requires quite a lot more than a single person can provide. A city must have a means of making decisions and settling disputes. Above all, a walled city must have some degree of unity, a community. People have to agree that they want to live in such a place, walled in with other people. And walls are not built or maintained by themselves: they are expensive and time-consuming. In other words, **a walled city is a place where people coexist with others.**

When connected to the Jubilee, this is huge. It means that Hashem is saying that if a person would like to go without all the insecurity of relying on a relationship with Hashem during the Jubilee, then he can, instead, rely on other people—that people are, themselves, a suitable proxy for a relationship with Hashem. The archetypal walled city in ancient Israel was, of course, Jerusalem - a name that refers to "shalem", meaning completeness. The Torah considers life in a unified community to be fulfilled and whole. After all, every person has a soul on loan from Hashem, so relating to others is relating to their divine souls. And when we find sufficient common ground within an entire city so that we are able to build together, we have achieved a direct relationship with Hashem.

The Torah reminds all of us that we need that connection, community and unity, as a fundamental aspect of building love with others.

14 HAPPINESS FOR OTHERS

One of the hardest things to do is to be happy for other people.

Morally, the founding document of Western Civilization (the Torah) tells of one brother killing another (Cain and Hevel). Then brothers who go their separate ways (Yitzhak and Ishmael), and show open hatred of one another bordering on violence (Yaakov and Esav). Yosef is sold into slavery by his brothers. The situation improves as Yosef's sons, Ephraim and Menasseh are the first brothers in the Torah who are not jealous of the other's success.

Finally comes Moshe and Aharon, brothers who are openly joyous when their sibling has done well. And it is with these two brothers that an extended tribe is ready to become a people that openly aim to be a Light unto the Nations.

The message is simple enough, and yet seemingly has to be relearned time and again: we should reject *schadenfreude*, and instead always root for everyone to do well. This is bitterly hard to do, especially when others have achieved where one might have failed – in marriage or children or business or any other endeavor in life.

Economically, celebrating the successes of others is equally important. Capitalism requires the freedom to exchange money, goods and services on terms that are acceptable to both parties. Which means that in any transaction, both sides reckon they got a good deal. When people start worrying that the other side got "too good a deal," then it becomes a barrier to smart business. In actuality, what *should* matter is whether a transaction is acceptable to each party. But once people start worrying about the other guy doing too well, then envy leads us to prefer doing nothing at all.

Economic envy, just like jealousy between brothers, is a slow and sure poison. It leads to a society that justifies "Might Makes Right," a road that starts with crony capitalism and ends with forcible redistribution of wealth, sold to the masses as "equality" but somehow always locking in the material, social and cultural exclusivity of those who get to decide what, exactly, "right" is.

Those of us who seek growth are not worried about other people doing well. On the contrary – we *want* them to do well! I want a successful China and Mexico and Africa. The richer other people are, the richer I will end up becoming as well, even if I might be poorer in comparison to those who work harder or make better decisions. In a world of freedom, a world in which the invisible hand and comparative advantage can come out to play, there are productive options for every person who is willing and able to work.

The Torah's tells us about loving our brother, and the lesson is equally true for all of mankind. We win at all levels when we choose to celebrate the achievements of others. When we maximize freedom, we maximize the economic, social, and moral fruits that come with the realization that life should not be a zero sum game, and that when someone does well by dint of hard work and ingenuity and persistence, we should be happy for them.

When we celebrate the successes of others and share their joy, we open ourselves to love.

15 FIDELITY

Labels are powerful things. We – certainly *I* – scoff at the idea of microagressions, but I don't doubt for an instant that a teacher can build up or devastate a student using nothing more than words of praise or criticism. By their very nature, labels are dangerous things: they lock both the accuser and the accused into the past, instead of looking toward the future. Destructive comments are particularly harmful because we should want people to have every opportunity to improve and grow and change.

Yet there are times when labels are absolutely necessary. Someone who murders is a murderer. As much as we want people to grow, there are red lines that we cannot simply ignore. The goal of much of society's customs is to keep people from getting too close to the red lines.

For example, in Judaism one of these red lines is infidelity. In Jewish Law, a man cannot stay married to a woman who he knows has cheated on him – the word the Torah connects to the suspected adulteress is *marah*—bitter. To try to limit even the opportunity to cross such a line, we avoid seclusion and even casual contact with unrelated members of the opposite sex. Bitter ideas eat away at the soul, giving us suspicion, and distrust. In its ultimate form, bitterness becomes rebellion, an open and unapologetic rejection of all that we are supposed to love. And while suspicion can—and should—be sorted out, open rebellion is a red line that destroys the exclusive love within a relationship.

16 MERCY AND JUSTICE

What role do mercy and justice play in the support of love? In the absence of these two qualities, applied in balance and fairness, anger, frustration and estrangement can result with no room for the emergence of love.

When there are legal disputes, a system needs to be in place to resolve them. Instead of thinking of strict law and mercy as polar opposites, perhaps it might be helpful to think of them as part of a continuum. It is possible for a legal system to be *both* merciful and just— just not at the same time and place. Here is how the Torah does it:

Thou shalt provide out of all the people able men, who fear God, men of good faith, hating unjust gain: and place such over them, to be rulers of thousands, rulers of hundreds, rulers of fifties, and rulers of tens. And let them judge the people at all seasons; and it shall be, that every great matter they shall bring unto thee, but every small matter they shall judge themselves.[19]

Adopting this system is more than a management reorganization. And it is also more than the simple optics: that people would *see* justice was done, because there was a process. The biggest and most important outcome that came from this organizational structure was that dispute settlement became a *process*, and a process which would change and grow as a given case moved up through the courts. Here is how it works:

The first "judge" would be one man in ten—an everyday fellow who almost certainly had a personal relationship with the disputants in his group. In other words, this first judge was the farthest thing imaginable from a High Court in a Distant Tower. He was more likely to be Norm from *Cheers* than the Grand Inquisitor. So when a dispute was brought to Norm, it is easy to understand that there was precious little actual law involved. Norm, after all, expects to have to live with the complainants as a neighbor—the last thing he wants to be is heavy-handed or put on airs. Instead, the approach would be "can't we figure this out between us?"

If the parties could not be mollified in this way, then the case would be moved up, and as it worked its way up, the settlement method went farther away from the informal mediation between neighbors and closer to a purer, absolute form of law that was handed down from On High. In other words, justice in this process was not about the law itself, but about a progression within the settlement of disputes that started with the language of relationships and mercy and mediation and moved, step by step, toward a much more impersonal judgment based on divinely-delivered legal principles. Ultimately, judgment from Moshe (or the top court of the land) could not be appealed, so if you insisted on taking a case all the way up, then you had to be prepared to accept whatever was handed down.

The Torah itself is quite light on the actual underlying law for any civil code, besides general statements of principles. But this specificity tells us what we need to know:

- In order to be satisfied, disputants need to be heard.

- It is not enough that justice is done: it needs to be *seen* to be done.

- The best resolutions are based on close relationships and mediation.

- Mutual satisfaction of the parties is more important than legal principles.

- Strict justice (the cold hand of the law) is a last resort, when every mediation effort has failed.

Note that a primary goal for the process to be successful is the closeness of the relationships and the desire to work out the issues. It requires a degree of caring, empathy and a commitment to maintaining the relationship. Ultimately when people learn to participate in a process that encourages these qualities, love has the opportunity to grow.

17 SHARED JOY

Hashem calls to us to be joyful; He knows that we have choices about how we feel, how we experience the world, and how we treat others. The best example of a celebration of joy is Sukkot, called a festival of joy, *simcha*. The Torah uses this word for Sukkot more than any other time of the year, which prompts the question: what *is* this Hebrew word that we translate as "joy"?

A quick analysis leads to the following gem: the very first time in the Torah *anyone* is described as being joyful is when Aharon is coming to see his brother Moshe, right after the episode of the burning bush. *Aharon is looking forward to seeing his brother.*

The importance of this cannot be understated. Cain

killed his brother Hevel. Avraham left his brothers. Yitzhak and Ishmael did not play well together. Yaakov and Esav quarreled and then separated. Yosef's brothers considered killing him before finally deciding to sell him into slavery. Even Ephraim and Menasseh, the first brothers who were not in competition with one another, were not described as being happy for the other. Brothers in the book of Genesis did not get on very well.

Aharon, however, set the standard for how we are to behave going forward. He demonstrated the essence of *simcha* when he reunited with his brother, teaching us that coming together with other people and with Hashem is itself a joyous event.

We are supposed to be happy for our brothers, and delighted when they do well. This is, of course, very difficult – and counter to basic nature (where offspring are always in competition for food, warmth, and love). It takes refinement to be able to stop thinking of oneself, and merely be happy for someone else. Think, for example, of how an older single woman feels when her younger best friend gets engaged. Or how a barren woman reacts when she learns her sister is pregnant. Overcoming our natural selfishness is extremely difficult to do – and the highest calling for a loving society. This is *joy*: not giddy happiness or lightheaded frivolity, but a feeling of deep and profound spiritual warmth.

Reaching this level is not easy. On the Jewish calendar, Sukkot comes immediately after Yom Kippur, the day when we spend the most time being introspective, examining our faults and resolving to be kinder to others, to seek to improve our world and that of everyone around us. Being able to be truly happy for someone else requires soul-searching and intense preparation.

But it also requires a highly developed sense of perspective and optimism. When Aharon comes to see Moshe, he is a priest for a slave people, a people whose god has apparently deserted them. Prospects are not good—not at all. And yet Aharon is truly joyful. No matter how dark and dim things may be, reunification is a thing to be celebrated as can life in general. When we are joyful, love presents itself in our relationships. We only need to open to it—with joy!

18 NEEDING OTHERS

Every relationship we have is unequal in some respect—whether we are talking about a teacher or a friend or a spouse or sibling. One person always holds more cards than does the other one; sometimes this imbalance shows up in one characteristic, sometimes in others.

That inequality is not, in itself, a bad thing. Indeed, I think it is a feature more than a bug: our individual limitations mean that *we need other people.* Man is not meant to be alone. Any person, left in social isolation for even just a few days will start to slowly lose his or her mind, fermenting, curdling, and finally rotting.

Inequality, of course, means that we are not level –

we learn from some, just as we can teach others. Financially the ties that bind are even tighter: wealth is defined in no small part by the ability to exchange money for goods and services. And many of our financial exchanges are not arms-length transactions at all—we integrate with our nuclear families, and we informally give and share with others in a social network that is defined by its relationships and may never even discuss money.

Our labor, then, is often not a simple exchange. My children help the family; in return I feed and house them, and my wife ensures they have clothes. We resist keeping score between parents and children, and, even more importantly, between my wife and myself. Relationships, even those that involve a lot of labor, are neither equal nor compensated in any measured or "minimum wage" sort of way.

When we recognize our differences with each other, and acknowledge that we all have a contribution to make, a special connection among us can evolve; that connection is created from appreciation, synergy, interdependence and commitment; these are the nourishment for love.

19 COURAGE

When we are in difficult straits, we may rationalize our plight all we like – and we often do just that – but the fact remains that in this world, it is *we* who are responsible for our lives, for the lives of others, and even for dealing with evil as and when we find it. We do not get to rely on a *deus ex machina* to get us out of any situation in which we may find ourselves. When evil emerges, it is our task, as Hashem's emissaries, to do battle. We do not have the option of merely quitting— that way, the way of those who lost their nerve at the prospect of claiming Israel as the national birthright, is what created the Ninth of Av as a national day of mourning for all time. No. As long as we draw breath, we must struggle.

The joke is told of an announcement from heaven that in 6 months, the world will be entirely submerged in water:

> The various religious leaders go on worldwide television.
>
> The leader of Buddhism pleads with everyone to become a Buddhist; that way, they will at least find salvation in heaven.
>
> The Pope goes on television and entreats the audience, "It is still not too late to accept Jesus!" he cries.
>
> The Chief Rabbi of Israel approaches the podium...stands silent for what seems to be an eternity...looks directly into the lens of the center camera and slowly but solemnly states, 'My people"...he pauses once again and continues..."We have six months to learn to live

under water'...

From the Jewish perspective, this is how we have survived 2,000 years of exile, of always being strangers in a strange land. When we are unfaithful, Hashem is angry. But we resolve to do better:

Let us search and examine our ways and return to Hashem.[20]

Nevertheless, it is a terrifying thing to realize that Hashem is not, as a father or a mother might, going to take care of us no matter what we may do. Our relationship with Hashem is a partnership, a marriage. And marriages rely on fidelity and trust and growth, the desire to always grow into the person that our spouse wants to love. It means that we always have to make an effort, or the love dies:

I called on your name, Hashem, from the depths of the pit.[21]

Nevertheless, the reality is that, however dire the situation, however awful and dark the world has suddenly become, it usually is not *quite* as bad as it first seemed. Which is why the Ninth of Av is not the whole year round.

Yet this I bear in mind; therefore, I still hope: Hashem's kindness surely has not ended, nor are his mercies exhausted.[22]

When we persevere, in spite of not knowing what lies ahead, we can remind ourselves that our love of Hashem, and His love of us, are always available and present.

20 BENEFIT OF THE DOUBT

When we judge that someone has behaved badly or inappropriately, the easiest route to take is to judge them accordingly. Yet, Aharon's story and how the sages interpreted his actions teach us a different lesson.

In Torah, Aharon is not fleshed out as a three-dimensional personality; he usually shadows Moshe, and he does what he is told, even when the situation is very challenging (such as serving in the Temple without complaint after his sons have died). But there is one very considerable exception: at the insistence of the people who have become fearful after Moshe had not come down from Mount Sinai when they expected him, Aharon colludes with the people and helps to create the golden calf.

Our sages could have excoriated Aharon for the sin of the golden calf. But they did not. What they did instead was to see his act in the best possible light: our tradition is not that Aharon was worshipping an idol, or that he was weak or afraid in the face of an angry mob! Instead, he was called a pursuer of peace, a man who wanted others to be happy so much that he was willing to compromise fundamental principles if that is what it took to make people happy.

The "reality," the data input, is the same either way: Aharon helped make the golden calf. The historical Jewish interpretation of that underlying fact is really a critical lesson for us, especially when tempers run high. Even an act that is tantamount to idolatry can be done for the right reasons.

It is hard to assume that others mean well, to give people the benefit of the doubt. But when we fail to do so, jumping to angry and bitter conclusions, our society suffers. On the other hand, when we seek to find the good, when we refrain from anger and nastiness, then we create the conditions in which people are most able to grow, to find common and positive ground, to reconnect with each other in holiness. And in love.

Thus, all of these qualities are connected to love in one way or another: they create the conditions for love, plant the seeds of love, enhance and deepen love. Love can bloom without them, but each quality provides a unique incentive and opportunity for love to emerge in our lives. Although we may not be strong in each area, life seems to provide us with many opportunities to stretch ourselves and grow; the opportunities to become a loving person, or a person who loves ever more deeply, are endless—learning to love ourselves, to love others, and to love Hashem.

---

[1] Terach left his father. Avram left Terach, Yitzchak separated from

Avraham after The Binding, and even Yaakov left his father and did not rush to return.

[2] One of Terach's great merits is that he was the first person to give a son his father's name (in this case, Nachor). That linking of generations might explain why all of Terach's sons (not just Abraham) all had offspring that became Jews. Seeing our individual lives as being part of a bigger historical tapestry is an integral part of what it means to be a Jew.

[3] People are the only "animals" that are instinctively attracted to fire.

[4] Genesis, 50:18

[5] Genesis, 50:19-21

[6] Leviticus, 23:22

[7] Genesis, 6:2

[8] Exodus, 2:21

[9] Genesis, 18:9 –One might be so bold as to suggest that when the angels come to visit Avraham and they ask "Where is Sarah thy wife?" it may be reproof: why is Sarah not with her husband? Why is she not also engaged in welcoming guests?

[10] Exodus, 1:19

[11] Exodus, 1:20

[12] Exodus, 4:25

[13] Genesis, 4:1

[14] Genesis, 4:25

[15] Genesis, 41:51-52

[16] Exodus, 21:22

[17] Leviticus, 25

[18] Leviticus,25:30

[19] Exodus, 18:21-22

[20] Lamentations, 3:40

[21] Lamentations, 3:56

[22] Lamentations, 3:21

42993909R00080

Made in the USA
Middletown, DE
19 April 2019